PERSONAL PEACE PROCEDURE

Workbook

Faith Bushby

You could go further in your personal and spiritual development if you used EFT on every negative experience you'd ever had. ~Gary Craig, Founder of EFT

ABOUT THE AUTHOR

Faith Bushby is a Licensed Massage Practitioner in the state of WA and has had a private practice for the last 21 years. She is a certified yoga teacher, and Biodynamic Cranial Practitioner licensed to work on all large animals. In 2015, she was certified as an EFT and a Matrix Reimprinting Practitioner.

FOREWORD

I see many people take Emotional Freedom Techniques (EFT) trainings to overcome a problem, and once that's resolved, they stop practicing tapping. Here's a simple yet life-altering process to be used with EFT that can make regular tapping a snap – it's the Personal Peace Procedure (PPP).

When I first learned to tap, I was so seriously motivated that I tapped night and day on the events that led to my illness. It worked as if by magic, but I learned from EFT founder, Gary Craig, that I could go further in my personal and spiritual development if I used it on every negative experience I'd ever had. I thought, "Why not try it and see what happens?"

The result was deep and abiding peace. I was a completely different person. I started sleeping better. I faced previously stress-producing situations with ease, and best of all, I didn't have to sit in the lotus position and meditate for hours on end. A few minutes each day devoted to clearing out and neutralizing one event in my past I wish I could have skipped (as Gary says), was transformational.

I encourage everyone who discovers EFT to do the PPP. This book will go far to assist you in committing yourself to the process. I look forward to sharing it with my students and clients.

ALINA FRANK

EFT Master Trainer

Personal Peace Procedure Workbook

For using EFT to become more self-aware, heal your past and have more fun

Congratulations on taking this step towards emotional freedom and greater self-awareness!

In this first section, you will be introduced to a technique called EFT, or Emotional Freedom Technique commonly referred to as *tapping*, a remarkable healing method that can help to guide you towards a greater personal freedom.

EFT is based on the same system as acupuncture but without using needles. It is a technique that improves the physical, mental, and emotional aspects of life as a human being. With a simple round of tapping, you can address a range of issues and calm the nervous system and restore the body's energy balance helping the brain respond in creative and healthy ways.

There is scientifically based research that supports the efficacy of EFT (Emotional Freedom Technique). The Personal Peace Procedure was created by Gary Craig, the founder of EFT, and this particular workbook is my interpretation. I have found it to be an exceptionally effective method for becoming more self-aware. After having tried many different modalities over the years, the Personal Peace Procedure has been the most consistent in bringing me to those aha moments.

In this workbook's first few pages, you will learn more about tapping.

This book has some exercises that will surely aid you when you feel overwhelmed or the intensity is too much. Practice these exercises throughout your day so that you automatically use them and you will find that you are calmer and happier.

I have a belief that the best parts of ourselves are what lies within. The good and the bad are all relative depending on what you fear or enjoy the most. Using this workbook will give you a perspective on all of it so that you can choose for yourself what you want and not be driven by past experiences and belief systems that no longer serve you.

There is a section at the end on beliefs. It is a way of coming at events from a different angle and it may help you discern those thoughts that are in-bedded in your subconscious and run your life without you being aware of it. And once you come to recognize the belief you reclaim a piece of yourself.

I am so enthralled by the clarity and knowing that come from exploring the deepest parts of myself that have gotten me to this point in my life—my younger selves that are steering me safely, in their eyes, through every thought. To me, it is the most rewarding feeling to see in my mind's eye those moments I have carried with me throughout my life connected to each other by a behavior or a belief. It takes my breath away how the subconscious has so literally carried out my every thought and feeling.

I have put this workbook together in order to share this passion. I would love to just be able to give you my excitement, but then you wouldn't know how to find it for yourself and that is so much fun. I hope you are thrilled by what you learn about yourself as you align with who you truly are. You are magnificent.

EFT Tapping Points

Please make the time commitment it takes each day for the next 12 weeks and you will be thrilled at how much better you feel and how much more you enjoy your life.

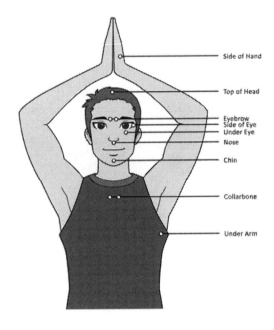

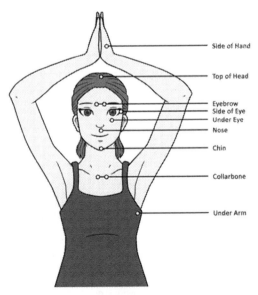

The EFT Shortcut Method

1) You will start by tapping on the side of the hand gently as you repeat the setup statement 3 times. It doesn't matter which hand you use to tap or tap on. The same for the other points as you move through the sequence. You can tap on either side of the body or both using whichever hand you prefer. Use 2 to 3 fingertips to tap with. If that is too jarring, you can rub the points instead or hold your fingers at the point and breath.

Each setup statement will include an emotion, the body location of that emotion, and a self-acceptance statement. The reminder phrase will use the emotion and the location of that feeling. There are many numbers of acceptance statements, such as:

right here, right now, I am OK;

I deeply and completely accept myself;

I honor these feelings that are coming up right now; and

I can begin to accept myself.

Use one that most resonates with you.

Example:

> *Even though I am feeling silly tapping, and talking to myself and I feel it in my tummy, I deeply and completely accept myself.*

> *Even though I am feeling silly tapping, and talking to myself and I feel it in my tummy, I deeply and completely accept myself.*

> *Even though I am feeling silly, tapping, and talking to myself and I feel it in my tummy, I deeply and completely accept myself.*

2) Then gently tap the top of your head as you say the reminder phrase.

   Example:

   This silly feeling in my tummy.

3) Gently tap on the eyebrow point, or points, repeating the reminder phrase.

   Example:

   This silly feeling in my tummy.

4) Next, tap on the side of the eye, or eyes, repeating the reminder phrase.

   Example:

   This silly feeling in my tummy.

   Now, under the eye, or eyes, repeating the reminder phrase.

   Example:

   This silly feeling in my tummy; or

   This silly feeling I have in my tummy.

5) Gently tap under the nose repeating the reminder phrase.

   Example:

   This silly feeling in my tummy.

6) Tap on the chin repeating the reminder phrase.

Example:

This silly feeling in my tummy.

7) Next tap on the collarbone point, or points, repeating the reminder phrase.

Example:

This silly feeling in my tummy.

8) Then tap under the arm at the level of the nipple while repeating the reminder phrase.

Example:

This silly feeling in my tummy.

Good job!

That is the sequence from first to last and top to bottom on the chart.

While that is the Basic EFT Shortcut, there are a few additions that you need to make it complete. The first is noting the intensity level or SUDS, which is the Subjective Units of Distress using a scale of 0-10, and then testing after you have tapped.

So we'll do it again.

So rate the intensity, from 0 to 10, of how intense you feel about starting this workbook. Write the number on the space provided.

RATE: _____

This is called SUDS (Subjective Units of Distress) level. Just so you know, the recording of the SUDS level will help you to recognize the change that takes place.

Now, notice where you feel it in your body and write it on the space provided. If you don't really feel it anywhere, just imagine where you might feel it.

_____

_____

_____

Start tapping on the side of the hand, saying the setup statement:

Even though I feel anxious about starting this workbook and I feel it in my_____, I deeply and completely accept myself.

Repeat 2 more times, tapping the side of the hand.

Then tap the top of the head saying:

This anxious feeling in my _____.

Next, tap the eyebrow point(s) repeating the reminder phrase:

This anxious feeling in my _____.

Then tap the side of the eye(s) repeating the reminder phrase above.

Gently tap under the eye(s) repeating the reminder phrase.

Tap the under the nose point repeating the reminder phrase.

Next, tap the chin point repeating the reminder phrase.

Then tap the collarbone point(s) repeating the reminder phrase.

Lastly, tap the underarm point(s) repeating the reminder phrase.

Take a deep breath. Have a drink of water. Now, from 0 to 10, rate the intensity level of your anxiety about starting the workbook. Write the number on the space provided.

RATE SUDS LEVEL: _____

Did the level of intensity change? Do you feel a bit better? Maybe more relaxed. Are you still anxious?

You can tap as many rounds as you like, or until you feel that something has changed or you feel a shift of any kind. Maybe the emotion has become frustration, anger, embarrassment, or you have an image in your mind of another time that you felt the same way. These changes are called aspects, and these should be addressed in another round of tapping when you have lowered the SUDS level of the original round. Be sure to keep tapping on the same emotion and physical location of that original emotion until the SUDS level is two or less. If it shifts aspects before that, make a note of it and come back to it after you have reduced the SUDS.

In other words, if you're tapping on the anxiety level of starting the workbook and it's an 8, and you start thinking about a deadline you have at work which is also making you anxious, write a note to yourself that you feel anxious about your work deadline and keep working on the anxiety about starting the workbook until the 8 has become a 2 or less and then tap on the anxiety about the work deadline.

If it doesn't change at all, drink some water and then check and make sure that you are being specific about what you are tapping on. Is it a specific time and place? Are you thinking of multiple things and times? Narrow it down to one specific event, feeling and body location.

GRADING LEVELS OF TRAUMA:

Alina Frank, master teacher, recommends grading trauma intensity levels from 1-4 in order to take good care of yourself and not re-traumatize yourself.

Level 1 being a small t trauma that may have happened recently and is a smaller event that you wish you could have skipped. You can work on it by yourself using EFT without re-traumatizing yourself.

Level 2 is an event that is apt to be a bit stickier in that it is still a small trauma, but it's possibly connected to other more intense events or beliefs and it would be easier and more effective to have someone else there to help. You might have tried to tap on it and you feel you just aren't getting anywhere and having someone else there would help you focus better.

Level 3 includes big T traumas like surgery, a natural disaster, an accident or anything that feels like a threat to your survival. It is also an isolated event that is not being repeated. You want to work with someone who has a good foundation and some experience and is skilled with EFT.

Level 4 would be an event such as an assault, sexual abuse, PTSD, combat trauma or an experience that you should not work on without someone else there that has had experience working with trauma specifically.

Craig Weiner and Suzanne Fageol who teach Tapping out of Trauma, an online class, go into much more depth about the differences between big T and little t traumas as well as the physiological responses and consequences.

Basically, trauma is feeling terrified and overwhelmed by something you cannot control. It is the awareness that you are endangered and the perception of a direct threat to your life, wellbeing and sanity. If you have any doubt about working on something by yourself using EFT, don't. Get help.

This is a self-help tool for the purpose of education and in using it you take full responsibility for your health and safety. So please be good to yourself and get help from a trained professional when you need it.

RESOURCES

Water is a resource and helps conduct the electrical impulses that make change possible. So drink plenty of water. Have water available whenever you are tapping and sip it as you finish a round of tapping.

Sit comfortably in a chair with your feet touching the floor. Starting with the right foot, rock slowly from the heel to the toes, feeling each part as it touches the floor. Then slowly rock back to the heel and keep going. Then, add the left foot doing the opposite. So while the right foot goes from heel to toe, the left foot goes from toe to heel slowly. Keep going. Breathe, and notice if you feel calmer. Your breathing should get deeper and you should feel more relaxed. Use this whenever you feel overwhelmed, panicked, or nervous. Think of a movie you've seen lately or a book you've read that made you feel uncomfortable, and while you're thinking about that, practice the foot movement as described above and notice how you feel. Practice two other times today and the rest of the week so that you are familiar and use this automatically.

Another resource to use when feeling intensely agitated is breathing while you notice your surroundings. Notice your breath, how the chair feels under you, and the feel of your feet on the floor. Notice the room around you, the colors that attract your attention, how your clothes feel against your skin, the sounds you hear, and then notice your breathing again. You can use this breathing while rocking your feet on the floor.

Before you begin a session, close your eyes and take a breath, to the count of 6, into your heart and then exhale, again to the count of 6, as though breathing through your heart. Repeat 6 times. Let whatever comes into your mind.

Make a list of the things in your life that make you feel safe, calm, and give you strength. It could be any hobby, book, people, music, place, or activity that cheers you up. What is your greatest inner resource?

Here is an exercise that was introduced in a workshop that I took with Alina Frank:

Imagine you enter a house that's familiar, safe and comfortable. You find a doorway that leads you to a moving walkway. You take the walkway to a building that has the word "Library" on it. You go in and you sit down. You ask, "If my intuitive mind had a color, what would it be?" You will write down the answers you get and then continue with "if it had a smell, an image, a feeling, a sound," and then finally, "if my intuitive mind has a book it wants me to see..." Then imagine going back out the building, walkway, or home.

Have a list of people you can call and talk to if you get in over your head and want help tapping.

Take Level 1 EFT with an instructor that has been certified as an EFT Instructor.

Books that help you learn EFT:

- EFT Comprehensive Training Resource Levels 1 and Level 2 by Ann Adams and Karin Davidson
- The EFT Manual by Gary Craig

Online Resources:

- emofree.com – Gary Craig's Gold Standard EFT Training Class

- tapyourpower.net – Offers podcasts, consultations, articles, and classes

- efttappingtraining.com – Has an abundance of EFT related articles, videos, training, and certification info as well as EFT research.

- ppeacep.com

- https://www.aamet.org/

- http://www.eftuniverse.com/

Please be aware that we all have experienced trauma in our lives to some degree or another and that we all deal with it in our own ways. There are big traumas and little traumas and they can all be overwhelming. Please get help with these if you have any doubts at all about handling it on your own. Trauma means feeling terrified and completely overwhelmed, and the perception is that you are endangered by something that you cannot control. It is the perception of a direct threat to your life, wellbeing, and sanity.

EXERCISES

Day 1

Your name: _____

Date: _____

Date I was born: _____

Where I was born: _____

My parents

    Mom: _____

    Dad: _____

Where we lived: _____

_____

_____

    List all the places you have lived. Either the addresses or what you remember about them, or what you remember being told about a particular place. Writing the addresses down, or their descriptions, will also trigger your memories of events that took place in these different locations and these are the events that you are looking for.

_____   _____

_____   _____

_____   _____

Names of brothers and sisters:

_____   _____

_____   _____

_____   _____

_____   _____

Names of grandparents, aunts, uncles, or other adults that might have been close or guardians:

_____   _____

_____   _____

_____   _____

_____   _____

Names of spouses, boyfriends, girlfriends, partners:

_____   _____

_____   _____

_____   _____

_____   _____

Names of friends, peers, classmates, co-workers, bosses, teachers:

_____   _____

_____   _____

_____   _____

_____   _____

In the pages that follow, you will find different categories and space to write down events you have experienced. These categories include specific ages, times, places, and people and some may overlap. Some may not apply to you. Use the ones that are most resonant. These are events that trigger discomfort physically, emotionally, and mentally. You might wish you could have skipped them altogether. Write down the SUDS level and keep listing events.

Once you have written as many events as you can remember (you may have close to a hundred and you will remember more as you go along), write these down too. Tapping tunes you into memories and events that you may have forgotten over the years. Write down the intensity levels of how intense they are NOW when you think about them. Then, each day tap on at least one event, so that the SUDS level drops to 2 or less. You will notice that some of the events that originally had a high SUDS level may not have much of a charge at all anymore. This is called the generalization effect. By working on various events on different topics, you may actually be affecting the roots of a belief, much like knocking the legs out from under a table.

Personal Peace Procedure Categories

The reason for multiple columns of dates in the Subjective Units of Distress Scale (SUDS) is so that you can go back and check an event after you've tapped on it or even tapped on other events and see that the intensity level has dropped or disappeared altogether. Also, when you begin and have listed events for the first time, you want to measure the current SUDS level from 0 to 10 so that once you have measured all the events, you can go back and work on the ones that are the most intense. If you need more space, please add events on an additional piece of paper.

Once you have chosen the event that sticks in your mind most, for whatever reason, be really clear about what you're tapping on.

For example, you've chosen the event titled "2nd grade Art teacher". Before you create the set up statement, check the SUDS level of the emotion you are feeling now. Not the emotion you think you felt then. It is how you feel now about what happened then—that's what you tap on—and notice where you feel it in your body now. If you don't really feel it anywhere, just imagine where you would feel it now. The set up statement would be something like this:

Even though, when I think about that time in 2nd grade when the art teacher expelled me from class, I feel really mad and I feel it in my throat, I deeply and completely accept myself.

Tap until the SUDS level is a 2 or less. If the emotion changes to sadness or frustration or anything else, before the SUDS level has dropped to 2 or less, make a note of the change so you can work on it next. Same thing if the location of the emotion changes in the body or if it moves from the throat to somewhere else. And if you have a whole new memory of something else that happened that you'd forgotten until you started tapping, write it down and tap on it after you've gotten the original SUDS level down to 2 or less.

Events from ages 0 to 10	SUDS	DATE	SUDS	DATE
1.				
2.				
3.				
4.				
5.				
6.				
7.				
8.				
9.				
10.				
11.				
12.				
13.				
14.				
15.				
16.				
17.				
18.				
19.				
20.				

Events from ages 11 to 20	SUDS	DATE	SUDS	DATE
1.				
2.				
3.				
4.				
5.				
6.				
7.				
8.				
9.				
10.				
11.				
12.				
13.				
14.				
15.				
16.				
17.				
18.				
19.				
20.				

Events from ages 21 to 30	SUDS	DATE	SUDS	DATE
1.				
2.				
3.				
4.				
5.				
6.				
7.				
8.				
9.				
10.				
11.				
12.				
13.				
14.				
15.				
16.				
17.				
18.				
19.				
20.				

Events from ages 31 to 50	SUDS	DATE	SUDS	DATE
1.				
2.				
3.				
4.				
5.				
6.				
7.				
8.				
9.				
10.				
11.				
12.				
13.				
14.				
15.				
16.				
17.				
18.				
19.				
20.				

Events from ages 51 to 70	SUDS	DATE	SUDS	DATE
1.				
2.				
3.				
4.				
5.				
6.				
7.				
8.				
9.				
10.				
11.				
12.				
13.				
14.				
15.				
16.				
17.				
18.				
19.				
20.				

Events from ages 71 to _____	SUDS	DATE	SUDS	DATE
1.				
2.				
3.				
4.				
5.				
6.				
7.				
8.				
9.				
10.				
11.				
12.				
13.				
14.				
15.				
16.				
17.				
18.				
19.				
20.				

Events from Preschool, Day Care, Nursery School	SUDS	DATE	SUDS	DATE
1.				
2.				
3.				
4.				
5.				
6.				
7.				
8.				
9.				
10.				
11.				
12.				
13.				
14.				
15.				
16.				
17.				
18.				
19.				
20.				

Events from Elementary School – Middle School	SUDS	DATE	SUDS	DATE
1.				
2.				
3.				
4.				
5.				
6.				
7.				
8.				
9.				
10.				
11.				
12.				
13.				
14.				
15.				
16.				
17.				
18.				
19.				
20.				

Events from Middle School – High School - College	SUDS	DATE	SUDS	DATE
1.				
2.				
3.				
4.				
5.				
6.				
7.				
8.				
9.				
10.				
11.				
12.				
13.				
14.				
15.				
16.				
17.				
18.				
19.				
20.				

Events from College, Graduate School, Training	SUDS	DATE	SUDS	DATE
1.				
2.				
3.				
4.				
5.				
6.				
7.				
8.				
9.				
10.				

Events in the Spring	SUDS	DATE	SUDS	DATE
1.				
2.				
3.				
4.				
5.				
6.				
7.				
8.				
9.				
10.				

Events in the Summer	SUDS	DATE	SUDS	DATE
1.				
2.				
3.				
4.				
5.				
6.				
7.				
8.				
9.				
10.				

Events in the Fall	SUDS	DATE	SUDS	DATE
1.				
2.				
3.				
4.				
5.				
6.				
7.				
8.				
9.				
10.				

Events in the Winter	SUDS	DATE	SUDS	DATE
1.				
2.				
3.				
4.				
5.				
6.				
7.				
8.				
9.				
10.				

Events with mother or female guardian	SUDS	DATE	SUDS	DATE
1.				
2.				
3.				
4.				
5.				
6.				
7.				
8.				
9.				
10.				

11.				
12.				
13.				
14.				
15.				
16.				
17.				
18.				
19.				
20.				
21.				
22.				
23.				
24.				
25.				
26.				
27.				
28.				
29.				
30.				

Events with father or male guardian	SUDS	DATE	SUDS	DATE
1.				
2.				
3.				
4.				
5.				
6.				
7.				
8.				
9.				
10.				
11.				
12.				
13.				
14.				
15.				
16.				
17.				
18.				
19.				
20.				

21.				
22.				
23.				
24.				
25.				
26.				
27.				
28.				
29.				
30.				

Events with siblings and other family members	SUDS	DATE	SUDS	DATE
1.				
2.				
3.				
4.				
5.				
6.				
7.				
8.				
9.				
10.				

Events with current or former boyfriend, girlfriend, partner	SUDS	DATE	SUDS	DATE
1.				
2.				
3.				
4.				
5.				
6.				
7.				
8.				
9.				
10.				

Events with peers, classmates, co-workers, bosses	SUDS	DATE	SUDS	DATE
1.				
2.				
3.				
4.				
5.				
6.				
7.				
8.				
9.				
10.				

Events over the course of your life that you don't want to even think about or write down	SUDS	DATE	SUDS	DATE
1.				
2.				
3.				
4.				
5.				
6.				
7.				
8.				
9.				
10.				

Events you wish you had handled differently	SUDS	DATE	SUDS	DATE
1.				
2.				
3.				
4.				
5.				
6.				
7.				
8.				
9.				
10.				

BELIEFS

Beliefs shape our bodies, how we see the world and how we perceive our place in it, and how we relate to each other and shape our realities. Think a thought enough times and it becomes a belief. And then that belief attracts to it the proof that it's true. The way you see things is through the lens of that belief.

Bruce Lipton, a scientific researcher and author of The Biology of Belief says that you have power over your biology. Your beliefs actually control your genetic activity. And he says that the environment and our perception of environment controls our genetic expression.

As you use EFT on events in your life, you will uncover beliefs you didn't even realize you held. You probably have a good idea of plenty of your beliefs already, like: I'm not good enough. I'm stupid. Mom loves my brother more than me. I don't belong. Etc. You get the idea. This next section will help you work with any belief that comes up.

Using EFT and tapping, you will find that you see, feel, sense, and experience different events linking up because the same belief underlies each event and may 'prove' to you that the belief is true. This feeling of connecting the dots occurs because you have realized a thought you believe about yourself and may have for a long time. By coming to this realization or cognitive shift, you have rediscovered a piece of yourself.

When writing down your beliefs use your own words that resonate with you. Write them down and then rate each one from 0-100% true and date it.

Then, for each belief in the blank space provided, write down the events that you remember that substantiate that belief and rate that event in intensity from 0-10.

Then, pick the most intense events and tap on them until they are 2 or less in intensity.

You may be tapping on an event and think of or remember another time and be tempted to start tapping on that event instead. Stick with the one you started with, write the other one down so you can tap on it later and keep tapping on the original experience until it's 2 or less. Then tap on the one you remembered.

Belief Number 1:

How true is this belief? Rate it from 0-100%.

Rate: _____

EVENTS	SUDS	DATE	SUDS	DATE
1.				
2.				
3.				
4.				
5.				

Belief Number 2:

_____

How true is this belief? Rate it from 0-100%.

Rate: _____

EVENTS	SUDS	DATE	SUDS	DATE
1.				
2.				
3.				
4.				
5.				

Belief Number 3:

How true is this belief? Rate it from 0-100%.

Rate: _____

EVENTS	SUDS	DATE	SUDS	DATE
1.				
2.				
3.				
4.				
5.				

Made in the USA
Middletown, DE
01 May 2017